A Cinder
In My
Knee

A Cinder In My Knee

Poems by
Carol Townsend

Buffalo Arts Publishing

A Cinder In My Knee. Copyright © 2016 by Carol Townsend. Printed in the United States of America. All rights reserved. No part of this book may be reproduced or transmitted in any form or by any means without written permission of the author. For information, address Buffalo Arts Publishing, 179 Greenfield Drive, Tonawanda, NY 14150

Email: info@buffaloartspublishing.com

Cover photograph by Carol Townsend

ISBN 978-0-9839170-9-0

"...*how can I forget the verses written in my gut?*" Ikkyu

Acknowledgements

An earlier version of *Andersen's Fairy Tales* first appeared in **Voices de la Luna,** Volume 7, Number 1

Compton's Pictured Encyclopedia appeared on the poetry page of the **Buffalo News**, January 24th, 2016

In memory of my father,
Clarence Townsend

Contents

Cinders 11
Bread 12
Soughing of the Pines 13
Andersen's Fairy Tales 14
Inoculation 15
Farm Pond 16
Compton's Pictured Encyclopedia 17
Instructions for Monday in Summer 18
Summer Sacraments 20
Canning 21
First Kiss 23
Gallivanting 24
Ritual 25
First Date 26
Mother Was Right 27
Bird Man 28
Daughter 29
The Offering 30
Clarence Townsend Speaks From His Coffin 31
My Father's Farewell 33
The Violin 34
Luck 35
Deed 36
Ark 38
Special Thanks 41
About the Poet 42

Cinders

Can you hear the rain of pea-sized grains
sliding down the chute into the cellar bin?
The *woosh* of anthracite by the shovelful
pitched during twice daily feeding frenzy?

The roar of the furnace's opened orange maw?
In winter, pipes pinged as hot water sizzled
up the metal maze setting iron a-clicking
in all fourteen farmhouse rooms--

which also meant ash to be emptied out,
grit my father spread onto the drive,
bordered by the snowball bush on one side,
and on the other, a thicket of forsythia

big enough to hide a bus.
A warning in country quiet, cinders crunched
under tires, caught in work boot cleats,
the bane of mother's existence when tracked

across clean kitchen linoleum.
In time, a basement oil burner was installed,
blacktop laid, wider than the street
out front, more like a boulevard,

but not before I tripped.
I still carry a fleck of gray under the flesh
of my left knee, talisman of the fall taken,
proof positive of the tale I tell.

Bread

Every Friday, eight plump loaves
emerged from the belly of our black
and white enameled stove--
one for each day of the week
and one to be eaten warm, fragrant,
with hunks of butter melted in.
But then, Mother discovered
Wonder Bread, its red, yellow
and blue balloons proclaiming
"Already sliced!"

Soon after, on a nine-hour road trip,
my sister and I invented ways
to occupy ourselves in the back
seat of the old Mercury--
like sloshing saliva in our mouths
until it foamed down our chins.
Mother became hysterical,
sure that we were having a "fit".
Next, we discovered a new use
for the new bread, chunks pilfered
from packed sandwiches.
Just tear off crust, roll a piece
between palms. Spit balls!
Without the spit. Bomb each other.
Eat the evidence.

Soughing of the Pines

Hidden under drooping pines
and lulled by soughing overhead,
my play place felt safe, secret,
as I built castles and kingdoms
from needles and cones.

Towering over the garage,
these trees grew until Father feared
their height, the roots too shallow.
A windbreak row gone bad, he said.
Men with cross-cut saws soon arrived.
Metal squealed against wood flesh.
Sobbing, I slumped among stumps
and sawdust mourning throats
that no longer hummed with me.

Sixty years later, I stare at the scar
that slices across a soft spring lawn,
the diagonal where another pine pressed.
Its thirty feet toppled soundlessly,
no doubt, its roots wind-extracted
and I wonder about the tree itself,
if it ever hovered over a lonely child
as she labored on hands and knees.
How it was sawed into lengths,
hauled to the curb.
Was a single tear shed?

Andersen's Fairy Tales
Grosset & Dunlap, MCMXLV

She touches its water-stained
covers and bent corners.
Her fingers trace the vine
that climbs down the spine,
the crane that flies overhead.
The small oval of imagery
on the front board haloes
a sad-eyed child in clogs,
arms crossed upon his chest.
Inside: a crowd of castles,
angels, sages, a Snow Queen,
scowling talking tree and reindeer.
A sticker is stuck to page
ninety-eight, one of those
that once pasted
cannot be removed, memento
of her sin at seven - *borrowing*
the irresistible tome.
"The Marsh King's Daughter,"
"The Princess and the Pea,"
"The Little Match Girl."
Which was she? Who?
Each one was tried on in turn--
answers from the *adult*
world hidden on a shelf
behind glass doors
built into the fireplace wall,
miles from anywhere.

Inoculation

The child's elderly cousin,
the one not quite right in the head,
tended overgrown gardens in which asparagus

poked up through drifts of poet's eye.
Tulips and lilies-of-the-valley spread into the lawn
and poppies blared forth from among phlox.

This woman with the earth-stained fingers
offered her blooms with their stems
wrapped in wet paper towels,

and a layer of tin foil inside a sheet of newspaper.
Once these bundles were safely home,
the child filled a cut-glass basket with water

and arranged her trophies.
She spread the colored pencils, the ones
begged from her mother,

across the dining room table and,
bending over her sketchbook, drew every petal,
memorized each leaf with a ten-year-old's intensity,
even though she was only eight.

Farm Pond

The marsh that lay in the flat between
two steep hills had been deepened
into a pond from which cows drank,
standing up to their flanks in August heat,
when mosquitos buzzed and bit.
In winter, the water froze smooth.
A hole would be chopped, thickness declared.
We laced up white-leathered skates,
skimmed across icy skin that separated us
from bullheads in hibernation
on the brackish, green bottom
that had squished between hooves
and toes on hazy summer days,
when, every Friday morning,
the hired man carried a pole and bait
down to the pond, caught a half-dozen
of these catfish, lugged them back
in a metal bucket, gutted them
on the back stoop, to be pan-fried
in butter, a melt-in-your-mouth
delicacy, if you could forget frightful
tentacles, innards that stunk.
If you forgot where they lived.
If you were able to pick out
each tiny bone.

Compton's Pictured Encyclopedia

Door-to-door my mother went
in her robin's-egg-blue Plymouth,
lugging boxes of books,
"better than growing vegetables"...

World Book and Encyclopedia Britannica reigned
in our neighborhood, but armed with the gravitas
of a former teacher, she sold enough sets
to win a trip to New York City, sold even more,
and miraculously, a volume appeared
in our rural mailbox once a month

until the bookcase groaned under the weight of all fifteen.
While friends watched television, I read leather-bound
gold-embossed tomes from cover-to-cover
as soon as each arrived, looking up unfamiliar words.
In seventh grade, the teacher scolded me,

said "gossamer" was not a word, red-marked
my composition on the nature of angel wings.
In high school, no nun could stump me
with a Reader's Digest word-of-the-month.

The set moldered in my garage
until yesterday's recycle pickup, its pages
stuck together, edges foxed, spines mildewed--
no resale value for all that knowledge.

Instructions for a Monday in Summer

I.

Lug basket of damp linens
to grassy strip near garden.
Sling sheets over clothesline.
Smooth. Secure with pins.
Stand on toes, position
pillowcases.

II.

On hands and knees
weed rows of beets,
radishes and carrots.
Imprint pebble texture
deep into skin.
Note red dirt under nails.

III.

Repel marauding deer
by hanging stockings
full of moth balls
mixed with human hair
on the fence.
Avoid the septic tank.

IV.

Unpin laundry. Fold.
Bury face deep in shirts;
inhale the wind.
See the hawk swoop
across a cloudless sky.
Dream of city life.

Summer Sacraments

My sister and I stoop to pick
strawberries with sticky fingers,

reach for raspberries, rare and whiskered,
whose brambles scribble gibberish

across our wrists, stop to bomb
each other with blueberry grenades.

Scratches, torn sleeves, fruit war stains;
the bite of baling twine

against sunburned necks, twine
knotted through holes punched

in Prince Albert tins, now heavy--
coin to pay for deep dish desserts:

strawberry-rhubarb pies,
sweet and sour, corralled by pinched crust,

blueberry crunches, scooped steaming
into Corningware bowls,

raspberry upside-down cakes,
crowned with pours of fresh cream--

wine on young tongues.

Canning

When weekends days turned cold
and the sky appeared shockingly blue
between bending branches,
my younger sister and I gathered fruit
into baskets, our pockets, too.

Together, we washed, peeled, cored,
cut around worm holes and soft spots,
simmered chunks with brown sugar
and cinnamon on the old white and black
half-propane, half-wood-fired stove.

Clouds of fall-flavored steam rose,
fogging our glasses as our mother,
wincing slightly from the swelling
in her finger joints, cranked mash
through the metal mill.

Our father sampled every batch
from a dented spoon, tenderly held,
declaring this one better than the last.
Stacks of jars with sunken lids grew high
on shelves lining stone cellar walls

as apples and pears offered their flesh
to the heat and hiss and we went off
to college, to jobs. Each homecoming
ended with carefully wrapped quarts
taken back to Binghamton and Buffalo.

Last spring, no blossoms billowed.
Antebellum Baldwins, Greenings, Pippins,

Jonathans and Northern Spies toppled
under the new owner's axe, the hillside barren,
pavement where the tall pear tree stood.

First Kiss

In eighth grade, Henry sat in front of me,
a big-boned kid, his voice already low.
Henry scribbled. And he scribbled.
Occasionally, he dropped a pencil,
and with a lopsided grin, bent down
to tap my foot with it.
One day, his shoulders heaved.
I dropped my pen and he whispered,
Meet me in the cloakroom.

Amid the coats, hats, mittens, galoshes,
he choked out that his pet heifer
had been hurt by a bull,
would be sent to the glue factory.
But don't tell anybody that I cried.

Maybe it was a consolation prize
for what happened to his cow,
or maybe it was in response to the teacher's
breaking the board compass
across a friend's back for kissing a girl
last week in the same location,
but Henry bent over to kiss me--
a teary, tentative brush of lips.

Henry grew up to become a writer
of a weekly outdoorsman column
in the local newspaper. However
we never kissed again.

Gallivanting

Saturdays in June, the four of them
would pile into the car for errands:
the purchase of baling twine, a tractor part--
though mother and daughters envisioned
a clothing store, a flower shop,
or even the Jeffersonville Pharmacy.

Her father drove with one hand on the wheel,
avoiding highways, snaking along back roads
following old wagon paths around foothills.
With a travel agent's gusto, he pointed out
the same landmarks every time--
Ole Man Tulp's barn, the lighting-damaged oak.

When they ate at the counter in no-name places,
he struck up conversations with strangers,
ordered cherry pie with his coffee,
gulped black from a heavy-bottomed cup,
winked at waitresses, said he never ate desserts.

Her mother, who always asked for rhubarb
or apple pie with her tea,
would roll her eyes and run her finger
along the edge of the mug, checking for cracks.

Siding with their mother,
wishing to sit at cloth-covered tables
with proper silver and china--
back tables at the pharmacy would do--
the daughters said nothing, because secretly,
their father whetted their appetites for wolfing
down the world, the *real* world.

Ritual

On the kitchen table,
a striped towel spread
onto which my father lays
his little brown pen knife,
the milking machine motor.

Like a surgeon, he prepares
for the operation, his calloused
fingers cradling the parts,
little finger of left hand
curled. Immobile.
Organizing as he cleans,
he hums, more like a purr
from the back of the throat,
his pale blue eyes focused.
Do it right or don't do it.

If he had disappointments
in life, he hid them well,
lack of a college education
the only one admitted. He was
a man of simple pleasures
and rhythms--rise at 4:00 a.m.
Milk the cows. Work the fields.
Milk the cows. Watch the sun
go down over his land,
one hundred-fifty acres,
as far as the eye could see
in all directions.
Sprinkle pepper into warm milk.
Upstairs to bed at 9:00 p.m.

First Date

He taught her to ride the old mare
at the stables on the farm next door.
He was thirty-five. She, seventeen.
He smelled of Old Spice and risk,
smoked Marlboros. A *real* cowboy.
His eyes followed her every move,
and after her last lesson
he flashed that lopsided grin,
asked her out for Saturday night.

But before he could open the door
to his shiny blue pick-up truck,
her father appeared in the driveway
with both eyebrows spelling "no"
and a shotgun held alongside his leg.
Not a word was exchanged.
Cheeks ablaze, she ran back inside.

The next day, the town was abuzz…
"did you hear about the feller
who always wears boots? 'Ran his truck
off the pier into the lake. Drunk as a skunk.
Worse, he almost drowned them girls."
The gun was not loaded.

Mother Was Right

"Carol Agnes," my mother would admonish,
"you must move far away from here
if you're ever going to meet anyone."

Jimmy worked in the pizzeria
connected by black and white tiled floors
to his father's barber shop.
Its red-lighted sign, missing bulbs,
advertised hot slices, good to the last bite.

He picked me up after work
in his new convertible, top down,
and we drove along back roads
"to look at stars," he said.
He pulled into a field of oats
tall enough to tower over the hood.
We talked and laughed, but soon
Jimmy's hands began to wander.

I was rescued by the farmer,
whose flashlight beam bobbed
as he crashed through the grain,
yelling that he had had enough--
his prized crop was being ruined
by young hoodlums, night after night;

Jimmy panicked, threw the car in reverse
flicking every stinging insect
from its perch into the front seat.
Red welts as big as pepperoni
rose up on our faces, arms, legs.
We itched, we scratched, itched again.
In the driveway, as I jumped out,
I told him to bug off.

Bird Man

At five, I stood on the bench seat of the Mercury
with my arm wrapped around my father's neck.
We traveled back roads, took scenic routes,
windows rolled down. He pointed out hawks,
translated crow calls on the way to Jeffersonville
or Lake Huntington for baling twine, linseed oil
or haircuts in barber shops blaring Sinatra songs.

When my legs were long enough, he taught me
to work the pedals of the Ford tractor whose tires
were taller than me. I watched him predict weather
with nose up, sniffing the air. I learned how barn
swallows made mud nests and where brown bats
poured from trees at sundown.

After the farmland was sold, he strolled roads
surrounding fields no longer his. Cats trailed
after him, tails like question marks, paying no
attention to swallowtails, red-winged blackbirds,
wild canaries that swooped down--
and when he died, a pair of mourning doves
took up residence under the kitchen window.
I heard wings whistle in startled flight,
soft laments carried on the breeze.

Daughter

The funeral home closed at five.
I drove up at four-fifty,
my sorrow stuffed like dirty
laundry into a duffel bag.
It bulged at the seams
and I could hardly drag it
past the car door.

The Offering

Neighbors and friends crowd
into the parlor, but murmur and part
for Muriel, the cousin with wild hair,
unmatched socks, and fuzzy slippers
who shuffles to the coffin,
thick with roses and carnations.
She is mumbling to herself.

She kneels among the arrangements
and reaches into her apron pocket,
pulling out a nosegay: the lopsided
heart she made herself
of wildflowers plucked
from the dead man's fields.
Muttering, she tucks it gently
into his work-hardened hands.

Clarence Townsend Speaks From His Coffin

My nose is out of joint, off to one side,
broke by damn fools trying to revive me.
How I hate everybody staring, especially now.
And *especially* that no good weasel
of a funeral home director. Imagine.
Him having been able to see my privates.

But this box is solid, polished
like chestnut wood from our own trees.
The roses put me in mind of the American Beauty
I planted by our front steps – it bloomed red
each year for my birthday. July 4th.
No one more patriotic than me.

With all this commotion, 'heard that you'd arrived late.
Don't blame yourself, what with folks gaping
at you blubbering, the "favorite" daughter,
just waiting for you to throw yourself across me.
Believe me, I would no sooner be here
than pull a settin' hen off a nest.

Drive by the old homestead for me –
say one last goodbye to the land. *My* land.
Never worked for no man my whole life.
Not that I had it easy. Raymond, he passed at six.
Stiff as a board in the bed next to me.
Harold fell off a porch railing backwards.
Dead as a doornail before he hit the ground.
Pa up and died before I graduated high school.
Strangulated hernia, they said.
Ma went crazy, bribed me to stay
with a brand new Model T Ford.

Forget that violin. It'll bring you to ruination.
You'll never amount to nothin' playing barroom fiddle.
Ma favored my sister, Lulu. Loved *her*.
But I kept on working, taking care of things.
Even after being bit by a rabid fox. All them shots.
No one grew potatoes, corn any better.
Or produced milk richer. That was before
folks got all funny about butterfat.
Had to rid me of those little Jerseys, Guernseys,
Brown Swiss. A sad day, me buying Holsteins.

I was forty-five when I met Flo. Swept me off my feet
tho' I wish she'd shared my affection for animals
like those little flea-bit barn kitties
I'd sneak into the house.

Farming is just too hard these days.
Just look at that Woodstock Festival, half a million
people in our back forty,
cows out all over kingdom come,
helicopters landing in the lower pasture.
Blocking the view. Disturbing my peace of mind.

You ask if I killed myself, did I do it deliberate like.
Did I even know that the paper napkin was caught
in my throat up in that Liberty hospital bed?
Flo, she was late and I was feeding myself,
eggs and bacon. You know I was born lucky,
but that damn piece of white toast sure tasted peculiar.

Hell, I thought I was going to live forever!

My Father's Farewell

My student says she wants to paint birds,
not stiff, but ones that breathe

and I want to tell her about the great blue heron
that stood as tall as me in the middle of the lane

that runs past our farm, on the morning
of my father's burial, how its stare pinned
me to the steering wheel.

My father always said that if one listened carefully,
birds could deliver messages.

It held my gaze, turned, spread its pterodactyl wings,
and in the slow drag of legs over fields,
I received his final blessing.

But I don't tell her.
I hand her a book, one with a heron on the cover.

The Violin

In the back of our parents' closet,
pushed up against the far wall,
sat a steamer trunk piled full with old
drapes and sheers which, on rainy days,
became capes and veils for my sister and me.
Underneath, its strings undone, lay a small violin.

My father was a farmer's son, learned the trade
at his father's side. But he would slip out,
practice playing in the moonlit orchard.
He was eighteen when his father passed.
His mother forbade him to play, said,
"You'll end up fiddling in barrooms."
At nineteen, a country doctor lanced
his blood-poisoned left hand.
The little finger curved, withered.

When Mom was coaxed to play the organ
at church, he bought a double keyboard model,
which nearly filled the living room.
As she practiced in the evenings, he tilted
back in the recliner, closed his eyes, kept
time with his fingers of his right hand.

Dad died before his granddaughter's graduation.
A pity. On my desk sits her class portrait,
a pretty red-haired girl with a violin across her lap.

Luck

Her father found four-leaf clovers
which he pressed in the family bible,
so many that it bulged with luck.
She hoped some would rub off on her
but she was never the one to win
the door prize or the raffle.
The one time she did win
it was on a ticket her mother dropped
into a paper cup. The prize? A baby
blanket, and she remained childless.

After he passed, no one claimed the tome.
She saved it from the garage sale table,
tucked it away, *for safekeeping,* she thought.

Twenty years later, during housecleaning,
she shook out its brittle contents.
Clovers fluttered down like brown moths,
spun into the wastepaper basket's mouth
and as they twirled, she heard the cry
of victory her father would make
as he stooped to pluck a winged trophy.
Struck by remorse, she retrieved each scrap,
replaced it between yellowed pages.
All but one. Caught between two pieces
of glass, it now floats across her wall.

Deed

For the sum of eighteen hundred dollars,
on the 24th day of April in the year
one thousand nine hundred and sixteen,

the parcel bordered on the north by lands
of George Lybolt, on the east by lands
of Frederick Cugier, on the south by those

of William E. Hollister, and on the west,
of Horace Smith, one hundred-fifty acres
passed into my grandfather's possession.

The contract's crumbling and yellowed pages
cannot hold the muck and manure,
the brown cows grazing on sidehills,

the ten acres of corn in top gallon,
nor the botched surgery that caused his death.
His eighteen year-old son, my father,

built a barn into bedrock,
the dwelling on the foundation
of a burned-out boarding house.

On the side facing the flames,
scorched trunks of maple saplings
grew around the char, horseshoe shaped.

My father was buried under a mature maple
at the highest point in Evergreen Cemetery,
his plot aligned with his father's

in whose footsteps he had groomed soil
in the foothills of the Catskills
with a pair of percherons drawing the plow.

But one of them died
before seeing a man walk on the moon.

Ark

Charred ribs poke through freshly fallen snow--
swaying like a new-born calf,
the old barn lost its balance, fell in a flurry
of dark, identical flakes.

Like a new-born calf's, its body swayed.
Crisscrossed hand-hewn beams
released heady mid-summer scents,
alfalfa, clover, and linseed oil.

Hand-hewn beams groaned, memories
not of axe's edge, but of tender shelter,
the closeness of animal flesh, white winter
breath sighing through flared nostrils.

Not the axe's edge, but tender shelter.
My father would lay his head against a flank
as he pulled rivers of alabaster into pails
and arched streams into the open mouths of cats.

My father's head rested against those flanks.
His eyes closed, and he hummed--
his hands plied their trade like his father
and generations before his father's father.

He hummed and his eyes closed.
His knuckled hands would have clenched
around the arsonist's wrist
and fire would have blazed from his eyes.

The arsonist's hands flicked hungry flame
across the long vacant hull and the old barn
moored on the hilltop shuddered and moaned,
lost its balance.

The hull of the old barn moored on the hilltop,
iron-oxide-red landmark, icon
in the foothills of the Catskills, gone, gone--
charred ribs poke through freshly fallen snow.

Special Thanks

To the Lake Erie Poets for their support over the past ten years, for the poetry workshops taken at the Chautauqua Writers Center, to Marge Norris for introducing me to the world of poetry, to Ann Goldsmith for her keen eye, and to ryki zuckerman who assisted greatly in getting my poems out into the public; to Thomas Sist who encouraged me to write in the first place, and to my beloved husband, John Cofield, for his patience and enthusiasm.

About the Poet

Photo by John Cofield

Carol Townsend is an Associate Professor of Design at State University College of New York at Buffalo State in Buffalo. She was raised on a small family dairy farm in the foothills of the Catskill Mountains whose one hundred-fifty acres she roamed as a child. Her family's rural delivery address was Happy Avenue, Swan Lake, always an embarrassing revelation. Since she was used to having dirt under her fingernails, she went on to earn a M.F.A. in ceramics from Ohio University. *A Cinder In My Knee* is her first chapbook.

www.ingramcontent.com/pod-product-compliance
Lightning Source LLC
Chambersburg PA
CBHW030604020526
44112CB00048B/1245